Living High On Life

On Life

Derek Dean

I0145219

For information regarding permissions, write:
DGD Publishing, LLC
P.O. Box 25486
Sarasota, Florida 34277-2486
dgdpublishing@yahoo.com

ISBN: 978-0-9820133-0-4
Library of Congress Control Number: 2007940464

Printed in the U.S.A.
Printed July, 2008

PUBLISHING

Dedication

I would like to dedicate this book to my wonderful parents, Rita and Richard Dean, the greatest parents a kid could ever ask for. They did the best job possible preparing me for the many bad influences I was destined to come across growing up and my parents instilled in me the power to make the right choices in life.

I would also like to dedicate this book to today's parents who are challenged daily with a massive juggling act of working and taking care of a family. I know simply being a stay-at-home parent is a job not to be taken lightly, but it seems today that most families have both parents out of the house working, trying to create the best life for themselves and their children. There just isn't enough time in a day to do everything. I understand that, for those people who have children, most of your time isn't your own.

So, let your kids read through this book and get a better understanding of the topics I discuss as well as what I call the Levels of Focus. These qualities I talk about will help your kids learn how to avoid life's bad influences. If your kids have any further questions after reading my book, sit down and talk to them about these concepts. Once your kids put them into practice, they can change the world for the better, one child at a time.

Preface

My reason for taking the time to write this book is to reach out to as many young people as possible and let you know that even though society has made it okay to develop certain bad habits because "everyone is doing it" doesn't mean you have to give in to that pressure. Each of you will make your own choices regardless of how good your parents are at teaching you the right thing, or even after you read this book. I just want to add another wake up call from an outside source. Sometimes it takes someone else to say something important before it sinks in as the truth, especially if it's from another young person's point of view. Throughout my life, I've experienced a little bit of everything; in this book I'd like to share with you how I was able to live high on life and not give in to any of life's bad influences.

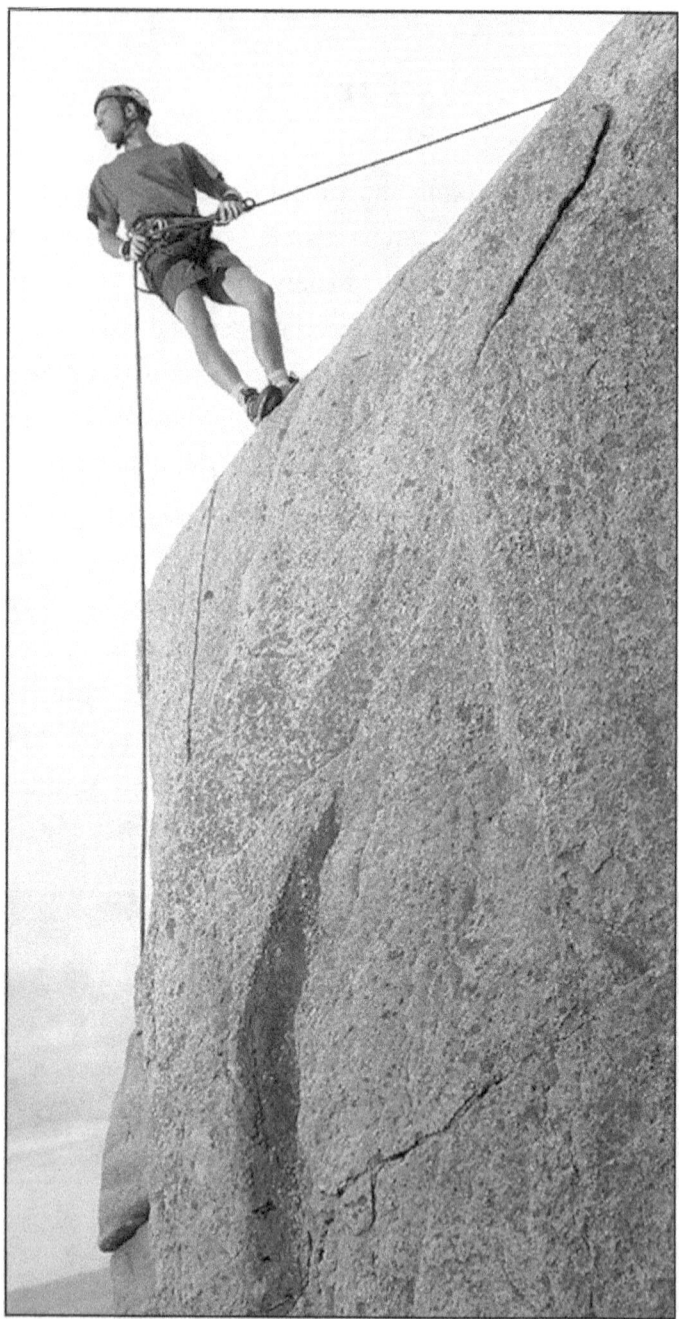

Table of Contents

Focusing on the Important Things in Life

Every day you make choices about what is most important to you. Focusing is the way you decide where to expend your efforts. Do you want to focus on your parents, your friends, your homework or TV? One big problem in today's world is that you can start to focus on things that are less important than the things you should be focusing on. Why would you give extra time, effort and energy to something less important? Because it's simply more fun. This is where you need to think; use the mind you were born with and focus on the most important things in life first. Then you can have all the fun you want.

I'm going to help you out by showing you how to use what I call the Levels of Focus. There are five main levels in all, and I'll explain to you where some things in your everyday life rank as far as demanding your focus.

The first level is simple: parents and teachers come first. When they ask something of you, there should be an immediate response to it without question or delay. I am sure all of you would love to just ignore that you've been asked to do something. You may respond by not answering at all, saying I'll do it sooner or later, or explaining that it's not your responsibility. Simply because either your parent or teacher asks you to do something makes it your responsibility to do it right away. Acting quickly to do what you've been asked to do is a sign of respect and it shows that parents and teachers are the most important part of your life.

The next most important part of your lives is school and homework. Without an education you can't get anywhere in this world. Paying attention in class and doing homework daily will benefit you more than you can imagine. I'm going to let you in on a little secret: the stuff you're doing in school now is the very basis of what you'll be doing throughout high school and college. Everything in school is a building block for the next year, so don't get behind in your class work.

Homework is the best way for you to learn the concepts discussed in class. For one, you're going over the work again which helps it to sink into your mind much better. You're also forced to solve the questions on your own without the teacher right there to help you if you run into a problem. The more you can solve problems on your own, the more you learn, and the more you learn, the farther you can go in life. This is why school and homework are important and are the second Level of Focus.

The third Level of Focus is staying nourished. Make sure you eat three meals a day at the least; it's also healthy to have a snack after school before dinner. Starting your day with breakfast is one of the most important things in a correct diet. By eating a healthy breakfast your bodies can start up and function better. Just like a car needs gas to run, you need to eat the right foods to nourish your bodies. You can't exist without food and eating the right foods is a big deal.

A lot of people think that eating whatever they want will be just fine, but that's not true. A good diet is not going overboard with sweets and what I like to call fun food: chips, popcorn, cakes and cookies, etc. Eating too much fun food can lead to obesity. So, try to stay as close as possible to the food pyramid guidelines; it's the best way to stay fit. Also, be sure to eat all of your fruits and vegetables; even those you leave on the plate because they just taste weird. Trust me when I tell you that all those weird-tasting veggies are acquired tastes, but if you just eat them a few times, they won't taste as bad anymore. You might even realize that you like some of them!

The fourth Level of Focus is keeping your room clean. You need to make your beds, pick up your dirty clothes, and put away the toys that you play with. No one wants a dirty room; you're just so lazy that your room gets messy and you do nothing about it. Here's the deal with your untidy room: the more untidy it becomes, the longer and harder it is to clean. The only solution to this problem is to keep your room clean all the time. That means beds made each morning, toys put away each night, and your dirty clothes put into the hamper when you take them off. Not only will you be happier that you took a few extra minutes to do this, but your parents will be happy too, and a big smile on their faces is a lot better than them grounding you because your room got too messy and unmanageable.

The fifth Level of Focus deals with any activities you're doing after school. Whether it's sports or some other type of recreation, or doing something related to the arts, it is very important to stick with what you love doing. Don't let the laziness set in. Make sure you show up on time and try your best in whatever it is that you do.

Those are the five main levels of the Levels of Focus. Now that you know how to balance the most important things in your life, you can decide what comes next. You can set any following levels yourself with things you enjoy like TV and video games or hanging out with friends.

Respect

Respect is treating others the way you want to be treated. So if you want to be treated nicely, then be nice to everyone even if you don't like them. It never hurts anyone to be nice, and you'll make a lot more friends than if you were mean to the people around you. If you show respect others will in turn show you the same amount of respect.

Respect is even more important when dealing with your parents and teachers. Why is this? They love you very much, and they are the most influential and important people in your life. Your parents and teachers will always be there to help you out in your life whenever there is a problem, as long as you are respectful to them.

Ways of being disrespectful include lying, talking back or ignoring the people around you. It is also disrespectful to go ahead and do something after you were already told not to do it. For example, if your parents said you're grounded this weekend and can't go to any friends' houses, you're disrespectful when you go across the street to play with your friends as soon as your parents leave the house for a few hours. Being disrespectful usually ends up getting you into trouble. The kid who disrespected his parents by going to play with his friend got even further punished after his parents found out what he did. Don't ever try to do something like that; your parents will eventually find out. That's their job and it won't be very pretty for you when they finally find out what you've been doing after they told you not to.

Respect is mutual. By showing respect you will receive it in return. In our culture respect is shown to those older or more experienced than us. In education, a person who has earned a doctorate degree gets more recognition than someone who has earned a high school diploma. We show respect for their expertise to anyone with a title, like doctor or general. Also, respect must be shown for people in power; the greater the position of power the greater the respect shown. There should be more respect shown to the president of the United States than a state governor or city mayor, and you should have more respect for your principal than you do for your teacher. I'm sure you spend a lot more time with your teacher, but like the president is the head of the United States, your principal is the head of your school.

Respect is an attitude, and at the same time it's a choice you make throughout your lives. The question you need to ask yourselves is: who really deserves your respect and who doesn't? The best way to go about life is to show respect to everyone you meet regardless of who they are or how they look. When others are not showing you respect or doings thing that are morally wrong, they become the people you can choose not to respect. Once respect is lost, it's one of the hardest things to regain.

In today's world people have begun to lose their sense of respect for others. We view today's society as evolved and advanced, but in truth only the differences in science and technology separate now from days long past. The fact is we have regressed in the most important parts of human culture. In the past, respect was gained through honor and honor was gained through courage and kindness. In today's world, however, most people simply look to fend for themselves and couldn't care less about other people. If that's not wrong then I don't know what is. You should always be looking to help anyone who needs it. This world will become a much safer place to live in if more people cared about each other, learned to share and showed respect to others around them.

Before you can truly show respect to another you need to respect yourself first. Self-respect is a sense of worth, dignity, honor, pride and self-esteem. The next chapters will detail what it is to have self-respect.

Responsibility

Everyone has responsibilities, and the older you get, the more responsibilities you have. Responsibilities are things you normally don't like to do, but in order to live they are things that need to be done.

Whether taking out the trash or handing in your homework on time, responsibilities must be done or there will be consequences. No one likes consequences. If you leave the trash and don't take it out, it starts to stink up the house. In the case of your homework, if you don't hand it in on time there is a consequence or penalty. Penalties are things in life you can always avoid if you're responsible. If your homework is handed in on time, you will be rewarded with a good grade. If not, you know the teacher is going to take points off the final grade. Why would you ever opt to lose points in something as important as school? The answer may be that you're lazy.

Laziness gets you nowhere in life. It can only set you back or cause you to pay a penalty. Part of being responsible means using the Levels of Focus and balancing what areas of your life are most important. One example of using the Levels of Focus to help you decide what's important would be if you have a big basketball game against one of the top teams in the league and your team really needs you to play, but you also have a report due in school the next day. If you're using the Levels of Focus, you know you can't go to

your game until after your report is finished. The best way to resolve a problem like this in the future would be to do your report when it is assigned instead of waiting until the last possible night. It is your responsibility not only to yourself, but also to your teammates to make sure that your report is finished before the big game day.

Taking responsibility for your own actions is very important. If you do something that is irresponsible like going to your game instead of finishing your homework, you have to realize that the next day in school your teacher is going to be very unhappy with you. Your homework won't be done, and when you do hand it in the following day, even if it's perfect, you're not going to receive a perfect score. Handing the work in late will cause your teacher to adjust your grade in an unfavorable way, possibly as much as a full letter grade.

The easiest way to be responsible throughout your life is to use the Levels of Focus and determine what needs to get done. You can then decide what things have the greatest consequences and work your way down the list to anything that has minimal or no consequences if it isn't completed.

With great power comes great responsibility. Where have we heard this before? Peter Parker (Spiderman) is told this by Uncle Ben before he is killed by a thief. When Peter finds out what happened, he decides to use his super powers for good.

No one really has super powers, but you can always choose to do the right things. You will gain respect from your peers by showing that you are responsible for your own actions.

Self-Control

Self-control is having control over your actions and emotions no matter what the situation. Self-control is a very important trait in life. Even in times when you're upset self-control can help you keep your cool. It can keep you out of trouble and even fights. Let's say the bully in school pushed you into a locker. The first thing that comes to mind is that you're going to get up and push him back or run away, maybe even cry. Using self-control you can calmly stand on your feet, walk over to a teacher and let him or her know what happened. If you're in the back seat of the car with a brother or sister and an argument starts, exercising self-control can help you stop the argument before it gets to a point where both of you get in trouble.

Discipline is related to self-control because if you learn a sense of self-control, you will be able to make choices about how to respond to a situation instead of just relying on impulses. Discipline is having the correct conduct by which you control your behavior and emotions in all situations. By exhibiting self-control, you can learn to make appropriate decisions and respond to stressful situations in ways that will be more likely to have positive outcomes. Self-control is being calm, cool and collected no matter what circumstances arise. Crying, yelling or screaming is completely unacceptable when you want something. Just show self-control and keep your composure. Parents, teachers and other people you interact with will be a lot more helpful to you if you can explain yourself in an even temperament, rather than raising your voice or crying like a little baby.

Later in this book I discuss some of the bad habits and addictions that plague the majority of people living today. The number one reason for the development of bad habits or an addiction is a lack of self-control. Being able to control your actions may be the single most important thing I hope you will get out of this book. If you're reading this book and you already have an addiction or bad habit, whether it may be sucking your thumb or smoking, please apply the principles in this book to your everyday life. It will make you a better person, free from the restraints of that bad habit or addiction. It will also help to solve the problem of getting in trouble repeatedly because you're not showing self-control when you know you should be.

Self-Confidence

Confidence is believing in yourself. Never say "I can't." Instead, say "I can." Never say "I'll try." Instead, say "I will." Everyone has great potential, but to tap into that potential and before you can accomplish anything, you need to believe in yourself. Whether it's things you don't understand in school or trouble in sports, having self-confidence means practicing repeatedly to work through your problems until you become more efficient at accomplishing whatever it is you wish to achieve.

Always work smart not hard. Working smart means maximizing the benefit with the least amount of time put in. If you continue to work on something the wrong way and do not get any benefit from it, that would be working hard. To work smart you need to have perfect practice, which means doing everything the correct way and getting the most out of the time you put in. Time plus effort will equal increased skill and proficiency in anything you put your mind to.

It is important to have confidence whenever you complete a task, whether that task is work related or not. Confidence is usually developed through practice. When you practice anything enough you get to a point where you're near perfect at it. At this point confidence takes over whenever you perform that practiced thing. Let's take free-throw shooting for example. In basketball, shooters who are confident will make a higher percentage of their shots in the long run.

Base running is another example. In baseball to be an effective base runner, you need to be able to put your head down and concentrate on running as fast as you can to the next base as soon as the pitcher starts his motion toward home plate. If the catcher is any good he'll throw you out. I can't guarantee you'll be safe sliding into a base, nor can I guarantee you will shoot over 80% from the free-throw line, but be assured if you're confident your results will show it.

Not only is confidence necessary to effectively do things in life, but it also reflects your self-image. The way you perceive yourself and the way you feel other people perceive you can either boost or break down your self-confidence. To have high self-confidence you first need to believe in yourself. Confidence is facing every problem that arises with a positive outlook and believing you will eventually find a solution. Don't let other people get you down. Don't even listen to people who tell you that you can't do something that you want to do. Just ignore them and continue working towards your goal. Remember, if you believe in yourself then anything is possible.

Personal Hygiene

I'm sure you've heard the statement "cleanliness is next to godliness" before. Even though this book isn't really about God, he always seems to pop up everywhere anyway, doesn't he? Cleanliness is basically having the correct personal hygiene. You should have a set routine that includes showering at least once a day, putting on deodorant at least once a day, brushing your teeth at least twice a day, washing your hands after you use the bathroom and before eating, putting on clean clothes every day and washing dirty clothes at least once a week.

Personal hygiene is not only important for you,

but it also affects those people around you. If you don't wash up, brush your teeth, put deodorant on and take showers or baths, then you'll start to stink. I'm sure you don't want to stink because you care about yourself, and because others will not even want to come close to you if you smell bad. That means not making friends or being involved in any kind of games.

Other things that are affected by having bad personal hygiene may include pimples on your face and body and cavities on your teeth. Yuck! No one wants pimples or cavities! Pimples make us look bad. Getting cavities means having tooth decay. That makes parts of your teeth sensitive, so it's hard to eat cold ice cream or hot soup. Cavities require lots of trips to the dentist to get them filled and that hurts. These things may happen even if you have good personal hygiene, but you're a lot less likely to get either if you keep up with your personal hygiene. It may be a pain to do all this stuff, but trust me, it's definitely worth the time spent.

Avoiding Life's Bad Influences

Life is full of bad influences, a lot of which are also habit forming. The rest of this book is going to address a good number of these habit forming bad influences that have a knack for finding ways into your life. Only you have the power to say "No" to all of life's bad habits and influences, whether it's smoking and drinking or using drugs and steroids. Take what you've learned from the first few chapters in this book and use the information as your weapons against all of life's bad influences. You will know when you run into a bad influence if you have to ask yourself questions like:

"Will my parents approve of this action?" "Am I going

to get hurt doing this?" or "What will people think if they found out I did this?" Bad influences adversely affect you and the people around you.

Developing bad habits by giving in to the influences are the hardest habits to break. Once down the path of life's bad influences, forever down that path will you walk. If you develop a bad habit and later want to break it, not only will it be hard initially, but there will always be a burning sensation inside you. You will have to fight that urge the rest of your life in order to not begin the same bad habit over again.

You will be influenced by all sorts of things like your parents, friends, the media, commercial advertise-ments and also religious beliefs. The important thing is to understand how these influences affect your life. Some influences, like saving money, having a positive outlook on life, or helping out anyone who needs it, have positive effects which are good to copy and adopt. Other influences can have adverse effects and should be avoided at all costs. I will try my best to cover those bad influences throughout the rest of this book, so you are able to recognize and resist their temptation when-ever you come across them in your own life.

By now you've learned to respect the decisions you make as well as those of the other people around you. You now have self-confidence and are responsible enough to have control over your own actions. If you don't, then please go back and reread the beginning of this book till you fully understand all those concepts. Only then will you truly have the power to resist temptation and the social pressures which are associated with a lot of life's bad influences.

If you feel confident that you have mastered the moral qualities of respect, responsibility, self-confidence and self-control, move on to learn exactly what all these bad influences are and why you should never be influenced by them.

Talking Back to Parents & Using Bad Words

I know you all love your parents very much, so when they ask you to do something for them don't talk back. What I mean is, if they ask you to clean your room, turn off the television, come to dinner, or take out the trash, don't tell them "No" or "I'll get to it in five minutes."

Be responsible and do what they asked without talking back. Say "Yes Mom" or "Yes Dad," and immediately take care of what they asked you to do without procrastinating. "Please" and "Thank you" are magic words. Whenever you want something say "Please," and whenever you receive something say "Thank you."

Whenever you do something to help someone out they will thank you for your help. The reply to that is "You're welcome." Now you're on your way to learning the right way to speak to people and how they should respond to you.

In today's world, you are exposed to bad words at a very early age. You can experience bad words coming from the TV, songs played on the radio, music on CDs, and from the people all around you. While you may hear many bad words during the course of a day, that doesn't mean you should incorporate them into the words you use to speak and express yourself. Bad words aren't even the worst kind of words; there are words called "swears." These are very bad words, and should never be used. I can't even write them in this book they're so bad, so speak with your parents about which words they consider swear words and don't ever use them. Try to express yourselves in less offensive ways.

Bad words include putting someone down or calling them names, as well as words used to express anger. Some examples of bad words are stupid, dummy, idiot and moron. Instead of saying these bad words, you may choose better words to express the same feeling such as ignorant, naive, uninformed or uneducated. Using bad words will not only offend other people, but it will also cause them to think you don't know any better. It's important to remember if you don't have anything nice to say, don't say anything at all. There will always be more pleasant ways of speaking. Try and develop a vocabulary with the least number of bad or offensive words as possible.

Pressures to do Well in School

Everyone feels pressure to do well in school from their parents, teachers and even themselves. Every grade you get is a small piece of a much larger goal. At the end of each year those grades are set in stone. Throughout your high school years and into your college ones, grades are the only way to see how you are progressing. If you're doing well you are getting As and Bs, but if you're not doing so well you're getting a few Cs, and if you're not doing well at all you're getting Ds and Fs. Even though your mind is always on doing the best possible in school, your life tends to complicate things. Here's where you need to use the Levels of Focus and make sure that when things come up you're prepared and have the time allotted to complete all of your school work. Then you'll have time for sports, friends, video games and any other fun you may want to have after school.

If ever there is a year that you didn't fare as well as you would have liked, no worries. Just make sure to work even harder the next year and it will all balance out. You'll be fine by the time the end of senior year approaches. If you're still not improving there are things you can do to get the most out of school. You have instructors or tutors you can meet with before or after school to make sure you understand whatever it is that's not being understood when you read through the class work yourself. These are people, along with your parents, who can aid you in the areas where you require help.

What is the biggest reason to do well in school? Getting into college is by far the biggest reason to do well in school. And, getting good grades in college will assure you a better job or set you up to attend even higher educational institutions like medical or law school. Grades in school and scores on standardized tests like the SAT and ACT will determine which colleges will accept you and which won't. When it gets to be that time that you're sending out applications to different schools, it's always important to realize that at that point in your schooling you've done all you can do.

If you are rejected by your first choice, it's not the end of the world. Consider sending out applications to three or more colleges anyway so that you can see what other options are available to you if your first choice doesn't come through.

Another really important reason to do well in school is when you get older you'll be comfortable with your reading, writing and arithmetic. All three of these things will be used daily regardless of who you are or what job you have when you leave school. Also science and social studies are used to understand things going on in the world and why certain things happen.

From first grade and up everything you are taught will come into use in your classes the following year and years after that. Don't ever assume that because you're not very good in a subject after one year of it, it's just going to go away. You're only human and it's completely understandable for there to be some subject in school that you just don't get. Don't be shy or afraid to ask for help. If that means letting your parents know about your problem and asking them to get a tutor, then do so. Trust me; it will never hurt you to spend a little extra time on a subject so you can understand it. Here's a secret to doing well in high school: if you're going to learn one subject well, make it algebra. You'll be seeing algebra for the rest of your academic life, not only in math but in science class too.

Dealing With Peer Pressure

Interacting with other kids is something you will do every day. Sometimes they are pleasant and the experience is a positive one. Other times you may be ignored, unwelcome or even picked on. Starting early in school you are thrust into an environment where there are a lot of other kids to get to know. They may be on your bus, in your classes, or you may have lunch and recess with them.

Kids generally find a comfort level with a few others who have similar interests, creating a clique. A clique is a close group of friends with similar interests and goals who don't like to include outsiders in the

group. If you are part of a clique yourself, I challenge you to be more open the next time someone tries to be included in your group. How would you like it if you were in their place? I know you'd want to be treated fairly too.

Another form of clique is a gang. Gangs are violent and detrimental to society. Gangs encourage members to carry weapons, and are often associated with committing crimes. Guns, knives and other weapons have no place in the hands of a civilian. Do everything you can to avoid becoming involved with anything gang related. Violence is never the answer to a problem. Any problems that arise can always be talked out and decided peacefully.

Being in school is tough enough for some kids; now they have to worry about making friends as well. Don't judge anyone based on how they look or because of what they like to do. Stereotyping is associating someone by the things they do or how they look. Avoid stereotyping at all costs. Make an effort to get to know everyone at school. Just because someone likes art more than sports or colors their hair black doesn't mean they are any less of a person.

Let me explain the seven general stereotypes used to describe everyone in school. "Geeks" are kids who are smart, may wear glasses, or are goofy looking. "Jocks" are the school sports stars. "Preps" usually dress nicely and are thought to have wealthy parents. "Goths" tend to dress in black all the time and may dye their hair red or black. "Outsiders" normally keep to themselves and don't really associate with anyone. "Blondes" are girls that just don't make much sense about anything, and there are some girls who are sexually promiscuous to get what they want. I won't mention what they're called here because it's one of those bad words I talked about earlier.

Have an open mind when trying to make friends at school and try your best to get to know everybody. Those who welcome you are the only ones worthwhile; don't worry about the kids who are mean or ignore that you're there. If someone is not nice to you, that doesn't mean you can't still be nice to them. Be the bigger person and don't let them get to you. Who knows, if they see that they're not affecting you they will more than likely stop being mean to you. On the other hand, if they know that you're bothered by them, it's just going to give them a reason to continue. These kids are called bullies. I don't know what goes on in the mind of a bully, but I can sadly say that you're going to experience at least one over the course of your time at school unless you're very lucky.

Whatever happens, make sure you are comfortable with the friends you make and the other kids you associate with. Try your best to not judge your friends based on appearance. It doesn't matter what's on the outside, because it's what's on the inside that counts.

Underage Drinking & DUI

Underage drinking is illegal. Even though that is true, I'm not going to be so ignorant as to say that it doesn't happen. In fact you will be confronted by alcoholic beverages the moment you enter high school, if not earlier. If you are underage, staying away from beer and liquor altogether is the right choice to make.

This is such a tough topic to talk about because society views drinking as a norm. So many people have done it in the past and are still doing it that the overall population sees nothing wrong with it. Drinking at any age is a huge mistake. What's wrong with choosing to drink fruit juice or tea? They both taste better, cost less and are healthier for you. Sodas aren't the greatest thing for your body, but like juices and teas they won't harm your body like alcohol will.

One of the biggest problems with drinking alcoholic beverages is the simple fact that most people usually drink too much, too fast, and too often. The key to drinking is moderation. If you're going to drink even after reading this book, please use moderation. If you drink a beer every hour or two you will still be reasonably fine afterwards, but if you try to drink three to six in an hour it is going to affect you. Does anyone like to throw up and feel sick or lose track of what is going on around them? I'm sure there are kids out there who are chugging down beers with friends just so they can look cool. Looking cool and being stupid are two different things. Think about it before you do it. If I drink, I'm going to throw up and feel sick; or worse, have the alcohol affect my entire body, leaving my mind unaware of what's going on around me.

Is that a trade off I'm willing to make? If you just use the Levels of Focus in this situation you can come to the conclusion that chugging beer is not more important than the chance of you throwing up, feeling sick, and losing your senses. I'm not saying don't hang out with your friends. All I'm saying is it's okay to chill, but be smart as well. Even if your friends are being stupid and drinking more than they should, don't be a follower. If you must drink, only have a beer every hour or two. You and only you can make the right choice of whether to be smart or stupid. If you think you can tell your friends what you've learned here, try to help them out. If they don't listen to that, tell them to get a copy of this book and read it for themselves. If they don't listen to you after that there is nothing more you can do. Maybe they will learn their lesson from unpleasant experiences and be smarter the next time they drink.

An older teenager with a driver's license risks the even greater problem of driving under the influence.

You are considered drunk after the second or third beer, according to the various state laws of alcoholic consumption in the United States. Find out by asking your local state authorities what applies in your state, so you'll know.

If you're ever drunk just try to stay where you are until morning, or call a parent to pick you up. I can promise you that your parents would rather know you've been drinking and that you need a ride than find out you drove home drunk. If you are underage, drunk, and caught driving your license will be revoked which means it will taken away until you become 18 years old or older. There will also be a monetary fine for being caught too. And if, God forbid, you happen to kill someone, it will be an experience that you'll never forget. You'll either go to prison where you'll have lots

of time to think about it, or you will have it classified as an accident and you will have it on your conscience that you killed another person.

Things like that change a person forever. It's something you can't ever take back. Death is a certain thing and once it has happened, it is irreversible. So please be smart whether you're underage and drinking or thinking about drinking and driving, look at the consequences and realize that it's just not worth it. Throwing up is the least of your problems if you lose your license until you are finished with high school. Wouldn't that be your worst nightmare? I know it would be for me. I can't even imagine not having the freedom to hop in my car and go wherever I need to.
I'm sure you feel the same way.

My first experience to a lot of life's bad influences mentioned throughout this book started in my freshman year of high school. I made the varsity basketball team and went to a lot of upperclassman parties. Almost immediately upon arriving at the party I'd be asked what I wanted to drink. All the choices were different beers. I knew drinking was wrong and asked them if I could get a Coke instead. They laughed at first, but then respected my decision not to drink because I was underage. Initially it takes courage to say no, but when you do, if the people you are hanging out with are truly your friends they will respect your choice.

Smoking & Marijuana Addiction

Very similar to drinking, smoking is a bad habit that is hazardous to your health. With each cigarette you smoke or hit of marijuana you take you are shortening the life span of your lungs and your overall life span as well. You need your lungs to function so you can breathe, and you need to breathe to stay alive.

Smoking blackens and damages your lungs, reducing their effectiveness. This consequence of smoking is not pretty. If you have to see it for yourself, find pictures of lungs damaged from smoke inhalation. Why would you choose to smoke now if it meant that in 40 years you were going to have a high probability of getting lung cancer and having breathing problems? Both of these things can kill you. You shouldn't be looking to shorten your life, you should be looking for ways to stay younger longer and live a longer and more fulfilled life.

Smoking produces the opposite effect because it shortens your life and causes health problems, including emphysema, lung cancer and cardiovascular disease, along with many others.

A cigarette is made out of cured and finely cut tobacco leaves, which are combined with other additives including nicotine, then rolled or stuffed into a paper wrapped cylinder. Both cigarettes and marijuana are habit forming and addictive substances. Nicotine is the biggest reason why cigarettes and tobacco are so addicting. It is a substance that doesn't function well with the human body. It instantly causes feelings of relaxation, calmness, and alertness, but these harmless reactions are just the mask for the true reactions going on underneath the skin.

Nicotine passes into the bloodstream and starts to affect the nerves in the brain within seven seconds of intake. This is the main reason for the strong addictions developed. The sensation from the nicotine as it slowly wears off starts to trick the brain into needing more; this is called withdrawal. Withdrawal symptoms are the false urges to continue use of the product so the initial effects don't wear off. They get worse the longer your brain has been affected by the nicotine.

Chewing tobacco is another way people get their fix of nicotine. Instead of smoking the leaves, they put crushed leaves in their mouth between their front teeth and bottom lip. The overall consumption of the nicotine is a lot worse than cigarettes since there is a constant feed into the bloodstream. How does it get into the bloodstream from your mouth you may ask.

Well, the leaves are rough after they are ground down, and as they are pressed against your bottom lip they make little cuts on the inside of your mouth to create the passageway into the bloodstream for the nicotine. Chewing this stuff is gross and produces a lot of extra salivation into your mouth, forcing you to spit it out. Swallowing such a potent substance it can cause even the strongest stomachs to throw up.

What is marijuana exactly? Marijuana is the name for an illegal drug made from the plant Cannabis sativa. The main mind altering ingredient in marijuana is THC or (delta-9-tetrahydrocannabinol,) but there are also more than 400 other potentially harmful chemicals in the plant.

Marijuana, also known as a joint, is made from the dried particles of the plant. The amount of THC in the joint determines how strong its effects will be. The type of plant, the soil, the weather conditions and other factors determine the strength of marijuana. The strength of today's marijuana imports are as much as ten times greater than the marijuana used in the early

1970s. This much more potent marijuana product increases physical and mental effects and the almost certain development of health problems for the user.

The best way to avoid smoking marijuana and any addictions to nicotine whether through cigarettes or chewing tobacco is to never try it.

From personal experiences, I can tell you that it's just as cool to say, "I don't smoke," or "I'm not interested in trying that," as it is to ask, "Can I have one?"

The people you're hanging with will respect your decision to not smoke. If they don't then do you really want friends like that?

Just use the Levels of Focus and ask yourself if temptation or peer pressure is enough to sway your self-control and the respect you have for your own body. If you learned anything from the first few chapters in this book then there is no way you would even think about picking up a cigarette or joint. Trust me; that's the best way to leave it. To this day I'm proud to say I haven't attempted to try either of them, and I never will.

Drug Abuse

Drug abuse is very serious, even more so than smoking or drinking. Drugs can kill you. You may never know when it's going to happen, but it could happen with any dose or overdose you take. There are many different kinds of drugs. Some speed you up, some slow you down and some distort reality. Each in its own way presents a false sense that messes with your normal way of functioning. Drugs come in many forms such as a powder, a pill, or a liquid. Ways to take the drugs include snorting, swallowing, or injecting.

I'm not going to go into detail about all the ways to administer the drugs, but I think the weirdest and craziest way to take drugs is when they are injected in liquid form. Addicted drug users who take the drugs often don't want anyone to know they're using them. They stick the needle part of the syringe into the white part of their eye. They do this so there is no scar left by the needle. Okay, if that's not crazy I don't know what is. I hate even taking an injection in my arm or finger tip; I think you feel the same way. Drugs are no good to anyone and can only get you into trouble, mess with your mind and body, or kill you. Don't do drugs and don't let anyone you know do them.

The most common illegal drugs you may hear about are cocaine (crack), methamphetamine (meth), heroin and ecstasy. But there are also prescription drugs such as Oxycontin, Demerol and Vicodin which are abused as well. The non-prescribed drugs are smuggled into this country illegally and purchased by people on the black market. The term black market refers to the distribution and purchase of things without government sanctions or taxes.

Drug dealers purchase the drugs from the distributors and from there sell the drugs to the highest bidders and addicts who are willing to do whatever they have to in order to acquire more of the substance. These illegal drugs are seen more often in the inner cities, but that doesn't mean you are not at risk of being exposed to them if you live in a suburb.

Illegal drugs are habit forming. Once exposed to

the pleasurable sensations the drug produces in the brain, the body can't resist the feelings created and feels the need to continue use. The prescribed drugs listed above are legal and are used to cure certain medical problems. When used either too long, too often or in too large an amount, these drugs also become addictive and can harm your mind and body like the illegal ones.

There are many more illegal and abused prescribed drugs than I have mentioned here, but I just wanted to bring an awareness to you of what is out there right in your school, town or city and how people are becoming addicts.

I was first exposed to illegal drugs as a teenager. Just walking out to my car at the mall, I was asked by some kids I'd seen at school if I wanted to try something. They were selling powdered cocaine. I knew enough to get away from there as fast as possible. I just told them I wasn't interested and continued towards my car.

Later that same year during lunchtime at school, I was confronted by some users of prescribed drugs. They asked if I had ever tried Oxycontin. I said that I hadn't and that I didn't care to. Just recently I was in a nightclub and saw some people using Ecstasy. I just tried my best to keep my distance from that group of people. As you can see, drugs are everywhere. You can't avoid meeting people who use them, but you can say no to drugs and make sure never to get involved with them or the people who use them.

Not only can getting involved with drugs mess with your own lives, but also the lives of the people you care about. If you do drugs and get caught you will be sent to jail. The mistake you made of trying drugs in the first place can balloon into a problem that includes your whole family and your friends, too. What will they think of you when they have to go visit you in jail or the morgue? They're going to be thinking about how you failed them as a person, and how they failed you by not being able to teach you right from wrong. Now that you're aware, don't ever let this happen to you. Don't have anything to do with drugs. Don't look at them, handle them and transport them. Never, ever try them.

Steroid Use

Anabolic steroids are a form of drugs and illegal. Athletes take these performance enhancers to help them run faster or jump higher. However, steroids can disturb the way your body normally functions creating many problems. Steroid users have been known to have reduced fertility rates, so if you want to have kids when you get older, then steroids are not for you. Do you want to be fat? Steroids may help in the present, but later in life your body turns all the muscle that was built while on the steroids into fat. We all know fat is very hard to get rid of. Steroids, just like normal drugs if used in the wrong way or dosage, can kill you. When trying to be your best in sports or any other athletic activity, just work hard and practice smart. Taking vitamins and lifting the right weight amounts can greatly increase your speed and strength without the use of steroids.

Athletes in most sports have taken steroids to get an edge over their competitors. There's a question of how many of baseball's all-time home run greats reached their record breaking accomplishments without using steroids.

Football is another sport where steroid use has been a problem in the past. Taking off tenths of seconds from your sprinting speed could mean the difference between a starting job and making millions or sitting on the bench and making much less. There will always be people looking to get an edge in sports. Get your edge through practice and hard work, not something harmful

to your body like steroids.

There is a strong attraction and temptation to try steroids, in the initial hope of becoming quicker and stronger. The simple fact is anything too good to be true isn't worth a second look. The adverse effects of steroids far outweigh the benefits. There are legal substances that have less threatening side effects which will produce close to the same results. In the future, if you are planning to use some sort of enhancement substance, check it out with your doctor first to make sure you'll be safe and to establish what dosages to use for your body makeup.

Dealing With Relationship Pressure

Relationships are very fragile when they first start. The best advice is to just be yourself. If they don't like you, then it wasn't meant to be. It doesn't matter if it's a new friend or your crush. When you find that special someone who you enjoy spending your time with, hold on to them. The easiest way to do this is to keep them happy.

There is no excuse for abuse in a relationship. Don't be reckless with people's hearts and don't put up with people who are reckless with yours. Don't ever cheat on your boyfriend or girlfriend. The best way to ruin a relationship you've established is to be with one person and then spend time with another. Communication is the key to successful relationships.

Be honest with one another and there will be a lot fewer problems that arise. Don't tell them things that would hurt their feelings. Think about what you are going to say and how they will react before you say it. People are different; one thing that may not bother you at all may really affect another person and could be the thing that ends a relationship.

Once in a relationship, there are pressures associated with doing things with the other person like spending lots of time together or having sex. How soon is too soon to have sex? Well, if you want to be safe, waiting until after you're married is the best time to have sex with someone. Let's be realistic: I can say whatever I want here and some may listen, and others are going to do things they may regret. If you do plan on having sex before marriage, make sure you use something that will prevent pregnancy. For a guy that means wearing a condom, and for a girl that means taking a contraceptive pill. Both countermeasures should be used because there is a 17% failure rate in condoms preventing pregnancy on their own.

If a mistake is made and you become pregnant it is a whole different situation and there are only two options: abortion or having the baby. You should both agree on which option to choose. Please use self-control and don't ever let it get to this point. I'm sure

none of you want to have a baby until you truly love the person you're with. It's also very important to make sure you have the money to pay for it. Babies are very expensive both in money and time. The baby is going to need your constant attention for the first few years of its life. Don't go about having a baby that you can't take care of. I'm sure you want your children to have great lives, and if you're not at the point in your lives where you can provide that, then you're not ready to have sex.

There is a chance you can become pregnant even though you took all the necessary precautions. The only sure way to prevent an unwanted and premarital pregnancy is to practice abstinence. If you really want to be smart then you'll wait till you get married to have sex.

It will be a lot more special with the person you plan to spend the rest of your life with. Otherwise you are taking a chance with some boyfriend or girlfriend who isn't going to be in your life anymore in a few weeks, months or years.

Sexually Transmitted Diseases

Now that you understand the importance of using protection to prevent pregnancy, I'm going to tell you another reason to practice safe sex. You could get a sexually transmitted disease, otherwise known as an STD.

I'm sure no one wants to get an STD if they can avoid it. In some cases, having protected sex can still lead to the transfer of an STD from one person to another because there are some STD's which are passed skin to skin in the genital area, such as genital herpes. Some STDs, like AIDS, for example, are fatal. Others can affect you so badly that if you are not treated immediately you won't be able to have kids later in life.

If you're serious about having sex with a boy-friend or girlfriend, go to a doctor and get checked out so you'll know if he or she has an STD and can pass it on to you. It's also nice for him or her to be able to see if you have any as well. I'm sure you agree with me that you'd be a lot less interested in having sex with a person who can give you a possible life threatening or incurable disease. Please make the right decision; use self-control and be responsible in your relationships.

Wait till you get engaged or married to have sex. Don't play with your life; you only have one.

STDs are the most common diseases in America, following the common cold and flu. If that's not a wake-up call I don't know what is. STDs are an infection passed on during sexual activity, close genital contact, or occasionally the mixing of bodily fluids with someone infected. This includes deep French kissing and oral sex. There are 35 to 50 different types of STDs. They infect around 3 million teenagers each year and 12 million in all; that's about 33,000 people every day.

One in five Americans is infected with an STD. They are contagious even in the early stages. This is dangerous in itself because with most STDs you can have them and not even know it. Some STDs have no initial symptoms, and your first indication of infection is a serious problem. The most common STDs are AIDS, Chlamydia, gonorrhea, herpes, HPV, syphilis and trichomoniasis.

Some are viral, some are bacterial and the last one is the result of a parasite that adversely affects your body.

AIDS (acquired immunodeficiency syndrome) is caused by HIV (human immunodeficiency virus). AIDS is passed from one person to another through sexual contact or the mixing of each other's blood. So be very careful. AIDS can be contracted from open cuts or sores as well as sexual activity. It is the fifth leading cause of death in adults under 50. HIV weakens the immune system so that an infected person has problems fighting off infections. As a result, infections that a healthy person has no problems with are often life threatening for someone with AIDS.

Chlamydia, gonorrhea and syphilis are all bacterial infections. They can all be treated with antibiotics.

AIDS, herpes and HPV (human papillomavirus) are all viral infections and there are no known cures for them. There are treatments for these; however, they only lessen the severity and length of outbreaks. Trichomoniasis is caused by a single-celled parasite. The parasite can be killed using prescription medications.

The only sure way to avoid ever getting an STD is to practice abstinence. If you're going to have sex anyway, please be smart enough to have both you and your partner checked by a physician before any sexual activity.

Losing Someone or Something You Care About

People and animals only have certain life spans and eventually pass away or leave. Things are lost, misplaced and stolen. Other things just disappear; loss is a large part of life. When around the same person or thing for a long time, you become emotionally attached.

You can't allow yourself to become depressed, stressed or angered when any of these things in your life suddenly aren't there anymore. The only way to deal with loss is to move on. Tell yourself that you had a wonderful time being with that person or playing with that toy or wearing that ring your mom gave you. We shouldn't ever live in the past; we need to live for the here and now and look toward the future. If someone or something has been lost, you need to appreciate the time you spent with that person or thing and find a new person or thing to center your thoughts on. Loss, in most cases, is uncontrollable; even though you may think that if you did something different you'd still have it, that's usually not the case. I'm not saying it's wrong to cry when you lose something you care about; all I'm saying is after you cry and get it all out don't dwell on the loss. Move on to greater and better things. They're out there; you just have to look for them.

There are five stages of grief and all are completely normal. Don't get caught up in any one stage because that's when problems arise that may cause you to do something irrational or be left in a dangerous state, like prolonged depression. These five stages were first written about by Elisabeth Kubler-Ross. They are: Denial, Anger, Bargaining, Depression and Acceptance. In denial you will first try to tell yourselves that what you know has happened isn't true. Then anger takes over and you become angry that there wasn't anything you could do to prevent what has happened.

After that, the next stage is bargaining, seeking ways to avoid the tragedy from happening. Bargaining is a futile expression of hope where you want to believe that the bad news is reversible. From there you pass into depression and sink into your misery, closing out the world and trying to deal with the reality. When you have finally dealt with the reality of what has happened you are in the last step of acceptance. Part of being able to move on with your life is knowing that what has happened was not in any way your fault.

Everyone in some way or another will have to experience grief over the course of their life. Loss is part of life and is sometimes very hard to deal with. I hope reading this will have made it easier to move on the next time you are forced to grieve over someone or something you cared about.

Depression

Depression affects a lot of people for many different reasons. Why would you get depressed? Perhaps someone close to you dies or moves away; you lose a special toy or sentimental object; maybe you get dumped by someone you care about or the relationship doesn't go as you originally planned. Maybe you lose all your money and have to declare bankruptcy, or you live in the past about things beyond your power to change. I can go on; there are so many things that people can become depressed about. The ways people sometimes deal with depression are by committing suicide, hiding from the world, abusing themselves, or constantly crying, etc. To avoid getting depressed it helps to realize that life is always unpredictable and there are crazy things that happen which no one has control over. Remember that there are a lot of people who love you very much and can help you cope. You have to be able to understand that what happened was not your fault or is out of your hands to remedy. You must find the courage to move on. Dealing with your feelings is one of the toughest things to do when you feel like there is nothing you can do to change what has happened. But by carefully dealing with those feelings, you can keep yourself from falling into depression.

Depression is characterized by mood changes that cause you to feel sad, upset, and hopeless for extended periods of time. Depression can have a significant impact on your enjoyment of life, your work, your health, and

the people you care about. It's more than temporarily feeling down, grieving or showing signs of low energy.

It's completely normal to have a wide range of mood changes from happy to sad to upset to pleased with things that happen around you. Being upset and sad, or feeling down all the time, or feeling you have no control to change whatever is bothering you could mean you're starting to show signs of depression.

Depression can be treated with success by professional counseling, using antidepressant medications, or a combination of both. In most cases the most effective way is to use a combination of the two. Normally hospitalization is not necessary, but in very severe cases it could be. Severe cases of depression can lead to suicide. Thoughts of suicide are not to be taken lightly. In these rare cases hospitalization and intense psychological therapy is necessary.

I recently had the misfortune of having a close friend commit suicide. I don't know for sure why he did it and never will. The scariest part of it was his friends and family never saw it coming. I had spent the weekend with him before the tragic event. I feel it happened because of extreme depression.

Depression is easily masked by a smile, but only the person experiencing it can truly know how he feels deep inside. If you ever start to feel like you're becoming depressed even a little bit, sit down and talk with your parents or a teacher about it. Depression is a psychological problem and is related to imbalances in brain chemistry. It can be cured a lot faster if diagnosed early. The longer you wait to get help, the longer the treatment will take.

Eating Disorders

People who are very underweight or overweight may have eating disorders. The main eating disorders are anorexia, bulimia and obesity. Anorexia is a disorder where people intentionally starve their body and remain very thin. Bulimia is a disorder where people eat a lot all at once and then force themselves to vomit.

Obesity is a disorder where people eat way too much and consume way too many calories for their body. In addition, obese people generally don't exercise much. The best way to avoid getting any of these disorders is to believe in yourself and how you look. Don't allow anyone to tell you that you're too small or too big. Have self-control with how much you eat and make sure that what you are eating is healthy. If you are unaware of what you should weigh, talk with your parents and get a doctor to let you know where you stand on the overall percentile for your age.

Anorexia is a life threatening condition which puts a very serious strain on many of the body's organs and its physiological functioning. It has one of the highest mortality rates of any psychiatric condition. Anorexia puts a harmful strain on the structure and function of the heart and cardiovascular system. People with the condition usually show signs of having a disturbed electrolyte balance, particularly low levels of phosphate, which has been linked to muscle weakness, immune dysfunction, heart failure and ultimately death. Anorexia does not affect everybody the same way, but the end result is the same: starving your body leads to death.

Bulimia is not as much about food as anorexia is, but it has more to do with deep psychological issues. It is a treacherous cycle of continuously binging and then purging the food eaten. Binging is the rapid intake of food that doesn't stop until interrupted by someone or when the stomach hurts from over-extension. This is followed by purging, the forceful act of vomiting the food just eaten. The cycle may happen several times a week and in serious cases these cycles may happen as often as several times a day. The consequences of this condition include damaging the voice, tooth decay, gum disease, digestive problems and potential death caused by heart attack or heart failure.

There is a big difference between being overweight and obese. There is a measurement you can use called a body mass index, or BMI, to decide if your weight is getting to be hazardous to your health. The BMI is a combination of your height and weight. If your BMI rates 30 or higher, the extra weight is putting your health in danger. Health risks include high blood pressure and arthritis. When you take in more calories than you burn off, you gain weight. How you eat, what you eat and how active you are, among other things, affect how your body uses calories and whether you gain weight. Exercising regularly will create muscle that burns fat, so the more muscle you have the faster your body will burn any excess fat. The simple cure for obesity is eating the correct portions of healthy food throughout the day and exercising. If possible, exercise every day or at least four to five times a week. If this doesn't help you should probably get in contact with a physician.

When it comes to your weight just remember the compliments you receive and forget the insults. I know it's not easy sometimes, but it's the only way to feel good about yourself. There will always be people who aren't happy with your weight; ignore them.

Discrimination

Discrimination is the different treatment of others based solely on their placement in a socially distinct group. There are five main types of discrimination: race, ethnicity, religion, age, and gender. The best way to avoid discriminating against people is to just treat everyone equally. Don't judge others based on appearances; first get to know them and then decide what you think about them.

Whether you're black, white, American or Asian, when dealing with race and ethnicity just remember everyone is a human being and has the same thoughts and feelings that you do. If you're Christian, Jewish, Islamic or believe in another religion altogether, remember that you're all praying to an almighty god in your own way.

Age is just a number that states how long you've been alive. All people mature at different ages, and just because someone is too young or too old shouldn't keep them from doing what they want to do. Gender simply states whether you are male or female. Regardless of your gender you should be allowed to do what you like without anyone caring. There shouldn't be any restrictions to a hobby, sport or job. Your gender shouldn't be a barrier in doing or becoming whatever you want.

Racial and ethnic discrimination has been around for centuries. You are lucky enough to live in an age where it is illegal, but that still doesn't mean it doesn't happen. If everyone does their part, you can hopefully be part of a society that does away with it entirely.

Can't you all see how silly it is to treat someone differently just because they have different color skin or because they were born in a different country and may do things differently than you?

Religious discrimination has been prevalent in society as far back as there have been societies. It shouldn't matter what you think about people who hold other religious beliefs and how they pray to their god.

They're just looking for the same faith and guidance as you. Just think about how your god would want you to act. God created all things and his intention was for them to all live in peace and harmony. Just because you may have a different view on what you do to please your god doesn't mean what another religion does is wrong. Both religions are pleasing god in their own way. Wars waged over religion were fought for all the wrong reasons and cost many lives. Even today, in the Middle East and other parts of the world, wars are still being fought over religion. I can only hope that in the near future people will be able to find some middle ground and put an end to the bloodshed.

Age discrimination is being treated differently simply because of your age. It exists at the extremes when you're very young or very old. Age discrimination for being too young may be experienced by those ages 1 to 25 and for being too old by those ages 55 and older. Sometimes it's positive discrimination like having a kids only menu, or having special senior citizens discounts. But most age discrimination is negative.

Some examples are making you wait until you're 16 years old to drive or 18 years old to vote and later on in life, deciding against hiring someone because they're too old.

Gender discrimination is the act of discriminating against someone based on their sex. Whether male or female, everyone should be treated equally. But that hasn't been the case. Women have often experienced a "glass ceiling" in the work place. The term glass ceiling describes the process by which women are barred from promotion by means of an invisible barrier. The craziest statistic I could find was that between 95 and 97 percent of senior managers in the country's biggest corporations are men. Let's work to change those numbers in the future.

Discrimination will never be entirely vanquished from society; some forms of discrimination are natural and help you understand your surroundings. When you meet someone for the first time your mind will formulate what you think or feel about that person in the first thirty seconds. Depending on how you process what you see, you'll judge that person based on their presence or posture. That's why first impressions are so important. Even though it's a natural response, try to wait until after you fully get to know someone before you make any final judgments about that person. There needs to be an understanding that everyone breathes the same air and has the same ability to learn right from wrong. Do the right thing and don't discriminate; it's wrong.

Managing Your Money

The most important thing to remember about money management is that you have to learn how to save money before you learn how to spend it. Today's world is all about advertising products to consumers, trying to get you to buy certain products with your hard earned money.

There are needs and wants in life. Needs are items that you have to have like a toothbrush and toothpaste. Wants are items that are nicer and cost more like an electric toothbrush. Depending on how much money you have to spend make a list of your needs and wants. Make sure to budget enough money so you can buy all your needs with some money left over to buy some wants as well.

It's important to remember with each cash gift you receive or paycheck you get to take at least five percent of the total amount and put it into a savings account. It's amazing to watch your money grow in a savings account when you just keep adding to it and never touching the money in the account. The special occasions which warrant the removal of funds from your savings account are the purchase of a car when you turn 16, and later on a house when it's time to live on your own. Even after that it's nice to continue to have a savings account for your future kids' college education, and things like vacations or investment properties.

Budgeting your money each month is the most important part to achieving financial stability. A budget is taking the money you have and dividing it up to pay for things. Let's imagine that on your birthday this year you will get $100. To budget that $100, take five percent out and save it; so $95 is left to spend on things you want. Say there is a new video game out and it costs $50. After you buy that you will have $45 left. Then say you wanted to buy a book and it was $30, and now you're left with only $15. Don't just find something to spend the last $15 on just because you have some extra money left over. If you ever have money left over put it into your savings account which will grow that much quicker. As a kid you may want to budget your money for clothes, books, or games. Later on in life when you have real expenses

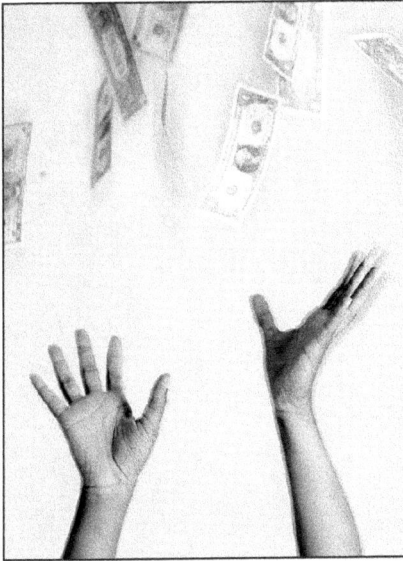

effectively budget so you can pay your bills in full and on time.

Your parents pay for a lot of your needs as a kid. Thank them for all that they do for you every day. Understand that when they buy you a new toy or clothes that they are sacrificing a chance to get something that they want for themselves. Don't worry about it though; you are the most important thing in their life and they are more than happy to make you happy whenever possible.

Being able to manage your money is a key to having success in life. I hope you all understand now how to budget and how to save. If you can master both of these things managing your money will be much easier.

Becoming a Complete Person, High on Life

Now that you've read this book, I hope you will be able to avoid all of life's bad influences and become a complete person, high on life. Throughout your life you will always have the Levels of Focus to be your guide in all of your decisions. Incorporate them into your daily lives to determine how important things in life really are.

Do not give in to a bad influence or start a bad habit because a friend has done so. Simply say "No" and try to help your friend beat it too. You can help her to also become a better person high on life, not some drug or stimulant. Tell her the difference is that being high on life is a high that never ends because you love what you're doing with your life and have lots of fun doing it, too. Highs experienced from drugs, stimulants or other fixes are only temporary and normally leave either permanent damage to your body or leave your body in a state of withdrawal. The more potent drugs will have both effects.

When you've decided to live high on life after reading this book, realize that it's a very contagious thing and that it is your job to spread all the qualities you've learned within these pages to family and friends. They may even be older than you, but if they see you saying "No" to all of life's bad influences, you may be able to get them to follow your lead. They too can live life the way it's meant to be lived, being a complete person high on life.

Combining the Levels of Focus with all you've learned in this book about respect, responsibility, self-control, and self-confidence, you will now have all the qualities needed to combat anything in life that comes your way.

Confront life's challenges head on; that which does not kill you can only make you stronger. Don't be afraid to make some mistakes along the way because learning from those mistakes will benefit you in the future. Always keep your head up, have a smile on your face, a positive attitude and never give up. Wanting something in your heart and soul makes it an accomplishable goal. Life is about focusing on your goals and realizing your dreams. Don't ever let people or circumstances get in the way of your dreams. Failure is not an option. Nothing is impossible if you believe in yourself, so never stop reaching for the stars. Every one of you has the power to make your own choices in life. Use that power and choose to become a complete person high on life, starting now.

Epilogue

My goal is to make this world a better place to live in and to do that I wrote this book with the intention of helping kids understand that they are the ones with the power to change our cultures future. In reading this book, hopefully you were able to improve in many areas of your life. Whether you were able to acquire moral values or avoid bad influences you have now become a better and stronger individual. The knowledge gained will always be your guide. By purchasing this book you have taken the first steps to helping change the lives of other people around the world. A portion of the proceeds will be donated to various charities.

Glossary of Terms

abstinence	*voluntary avoidance of sexual intercourse*
accusations	*a charge of wrongdoing*
bankrupt	*reduced to a state of financial ruin*
bingeing	*an act of excessive or compulsive consumption of food*
circumstances	*condition, fact, or event accompanying, conditioning, or determining another*
consumption	*the utilization of economic goods in the satisfaction of wants*
diagnose	*to recognize by signs or symptoms*
emphysema	*a condition of the lung marked by abnormal enlargement of the alveoli with loss of pulmonary elasticity that is characterized especially by shortness of breath and may lead to impairment of heart action*
exhibiting	*to show or display outwardly especially by visible signs or actions*
fertility	*being capable to breed or reproduce*
genital	*of, relating to, or being a sexual organ.*
hazardous	*involving or exposing one to risk*
incorporate	*to unite or combine as to form one body.*

influential	*a spiritual or moral force*
interacting	*to act upon one another*
irrational	*lacking usual or normal mental clarity or coherence*
knack	*a clever way of doing something*
moderation	*to lessen the intensity or extremeness of*
mutual	*directed by each toward the other or the others*
nourished	*to furnish or sustain with nutrients*
potent	*chemically or medicinally effective*
prevalent	*generally or widely accepted, practiced, or favored*
procrastinating	*to put off intentionally the doing of something that should be done*
proficiency	*advancement in knowledge or skill*
promiscuous	*not restricted to one sexual partner*
purging	*to have or produce frequent evacuations of food*
recognition	*special notice or attention*
restraints	*to prevent, limit, restrict, or keep under control*
sentimental	*marked or governed by feeling, sensibility, or emotional idealism*
significant	*having meaning*
stability	*the strength to stand or endure*
syringe	*A device that consists of a hollow barrel with a plunger and hollow needle*

temptation	*to attract artfully or by arousing hope or desire*
vanquished	*subdue completely*
warrant	*evidence for or token of authorization*
withdrawal	*the syndrome of often painful physical and psychological symptoms that follows discontinuance of an addicting drug*

Putting the Concepts Into Practice

Focus

What are the first five Levels of Focus? 1.

2.

3.

4.

5.

Decide the next five Levels of Focus in your life.

1.

2.

3.

4.

5.

Name five things you are going to focus on less?

1.

2.

3.

4.

5.

Respect

What is respect?

Who are the people you should be showing the most respect to?

How are you going to show respect to those people?

How can you make this world a safer place to live?

Responsibility

What is responsibility?

Name some responsibilities you have now?

How are you going to become more responsible?

Self-Control

What is self-control?

Why is having self-control important?

What are you going to do to increase your self-control?

How is having self-control going to make you a better person?

Self-Confidence

What is self-confidence?

Why is having self-confidence important?

How are you going to develop self-confidence?

What is having self-confidence going to do for you?

Avoiding Life's Bad Influences

Name the four moral values you
learned about in this book.

1.

2.

3.

4.

What have you learned so you can avoid
life's bad influences?

What are the steps you are going to take on a personal
level so that bad influences are never a part of your life?

1.

2.

3.

4.

5.

6.

7.

8.

9.

10.

Goals and Dreams

*List all your goals and dreams, then cross
them off this list as you accomplish them.*

1.

2.

3.

4.

5.

6.

7.

8.

9.

10.